THE SIMPLE THINGS

IN GOD'S HANDS

Carla Mewborn

THE SIMPLE THINGS IN GOD'S HANDS

iUniverse books may be ordered through booksellers or by contacting:

iUniverse
1663 Liberty Drive
Bloomington, IN 47403
www.iuniverse.com
844-349-9409

ISBN: 978-1-6632-3080-5 (sc)
ISBN: 978-1-6632-3081-2 (e)

Print information available on the last page.

iUniverse rev. date: 11/08/2021

CONTENTS

INTRODUCTION

Every believer should live a life of victory, in every area of their life. This book has been designed to help simplify the strength, the courage, and the ability to keep moving forward. Don't be discouraged, or find fault when you start reading this book. I want you to see the simple beauty of life, that our God gives us to enjoy each day. God talks from the raising of the sun, through the clouds, the wind, the trees, a general conversation with a stranger, our family or the moon. This pandemic has allowed us to enjoy the simple things of life.

"It is better to trust in the Lord than to put confidence in man" (Psalm 118:8 NKJV). I rather be in God's hands where it is safe, peaceful, and joyful. The people couldn't find any fault in Jesus, but they still crucified him.

I hope this book is inspiring to you as it was to me. I encourage you to get the word in your spirit. You must know you are in the hands of God. He will never leave you nor forsake you. We are a product of God and we are his children.

We need to spend time with God to renew our minds. I have spent night after night wondering what direction to go. Then God spoke to me, he made me realize that I have to stand up and shake the devil off. The word of God says, "But God has not given us the spirit of fear; but of power, and of love and of a sound mind" (2 Timothy 1:7 NKJV). The enemy is under our feet, do not allow him to have control over your life. God's word says "Greater is he that is in you, than he that is in the world" (1John 4:4 NKJV).

As you read this book, look at the power of God. You will realize that God has a purpose for your life. As you continue to read, I pray you learn to enjoy the simple things and find your purpose in God.

KEEP IT SIMPLE

For many years, I was the person who was just existing. I watched others enjoy their lives, celebrating, traveling, etc. I didn't know what direction I was taking in my journey. I don't know if it was heaven or hell. What I did know, I wasn't enjoying my life. One thing I had to learn was how to enjoy life in God's word. I had to learn to study, speak God's word over my life, and apply the word of God to my life. Dealing with family and friends, will teach you to change your approach on how to look at life. I had to speak positivity in my life. I am more than a conquer, I am an overcomer, I am a child of God, and my Father is rich. He has cattle on a thousand hills. Once, I learned to get those affirmations in my spirit, I became confident in the word of God. The next step is obedience. Obedience is the greatest way to please God. He will bless you tremendously. "Blessed are the meek: for they shall inherit the earth" (Matthew 5:5 NKJV). Satan wants to keep us blind, by the ways of this world so we don't get the rewards of God. I'm not going to say living for God is easy. His rewards are worth the suffering, sacrifices, and persecution. The greatest reward is to have heaven as our final home.

When we don't live to the full potential that God sees in his children, we are allowing Satan "to steal, and to kill, and to destroy" (John 10:10 KJV). God said "I am come that they might have life, and that they might have it more abundantly" (John 10:10 KJV). I believe as people we are not aware of our weakness. We don't want to look at our weakness because it will make us look at our imperfections. Our imperfections allows us to look at our truth. The truth isn't complicated. It is simple!

You ask how is it simple? We have heard all our lives that everything is in the word of God. It is, I am a witness!!! The more I read, the more I learn that everything is in the Bible. The word of God says "God is a Spirit: and they that worship him must worship him in spirit and in truth" (John 4:24, KJV). When we come before God with our imperfections or issues, we are acknowledging our faults. God will fix our imperfections and issues. We may not like how God fix those imperfection and issues. For example, I held a grudge against a family member for a long time, because they drove under the influence taking us for pizza and a movie. I had to learn that this family member was ignorant to his issues. Alcohol was the natural answer. God is the overall answer. We don't like to feel the pain of the issue. We have to examine ourselves, it's like looking in the mirror at all our imperfections which isn't pretty at all. We might be pretty on the outside, but we are a pure mess on the inside. Some people can see the inside, they know you are a mess. Our imperfections are like an old house that has been lived in for fifty years, the floors and roof are rotten, windows are broken or shattered, and the door fallen off the hinges. We still put on that mask of a proud look, and let's not forget the all-time favorite when someone ask you, how are you doing and you respond back, I'm fine. NO, YOU ARE NOT! How simple is that! People is going to talk no matter what. I'm not saying to have a pity party. Repent! "I tell you, Nay: but, except ye repent, ye shall all likewise perish" (Luke 13:3, KJV). You have to take the step into the right direction, and move on.

God will teach you how to enjoy the simple things of life. Which will build a relationship between you and God. God wants us to approach life with child-like faith. When you was a child and you asked your mom or dad, if you could have that doll or shirt? Your parents might have said, "Let's see how you behave, do good in school, etc. You knew if you behaved, your parents were going to come through. Well, that is what it should be like with God. We should have faith enough to believe that if we do what he ask of us, he will give us what we need and when we need it.

Enjoy God and all his creations. Stop making God and the Holy Spirit complicated. He lives in the simplicity of extraordinary power of our lives. He will teach you simplicity if you want to be taught. Enjoy the simple everyday things of life. One of my favorite things that I enjoy doing, is watch the sunrise in the morning. Here is a picture of God in his beauty. Thank and praise God every morning he allow you to see. "This is the day which the Lord hath made; we will rejoice and be glad in it" (Psalm 118:24, KJV).

BEGINNING OF A NEW DAY

What can you thank God for? Who did you talk to that you had been missing or crossed your mind? What did you see? Was it a tree moving in the wind, and leaned a certain way? Whatever way you saw God this morning, afternoon, evening or night. Share your thoughts, It's simple!

_____

_____

_____

_____

_____

_____

_____

_____

_____

_____

_____

_____

_____

_____

_____

_____

_____

_____

_____

_____

_____

_____

PROCESS OF CHANGE

As people we mummer and complain when things at work, church or in life has to change. We as people of God have to change to go higher in God. We complain, because it doesn't feel good. God isn't doing it the way we expected. We want God to do this and that but you not expecting to change. You want everyone to change around you. Sorry, to give you the bad news. The change starts with you!

We confine to what is comfortable. An example is you need a new coat. This coat is unravelling around the cuff of the sleeves, the bottom of the coat, around the edge of the pockets, but this coat is so comfortable. You dislike the fact of getting rid of it. You tell yourself you need to buy a new coat. You think of how comfy that coat is. You procrastinate to purchase that coat. Until, someone says something embarrassing, someone buys you a coat or you purchase it yourself. Once you start wearing that coat, you realize it is more efficient than the coat you had before. Another example, we see someone with their car rusted, two tone doors, interior floor is so rusted that you can see the ground. We will say they need a new car. Yes, they may need a new car. Do you know where they are financially? They might can't afford that car just yet. That is how change works as well. We have to get where we are ready for the change. If you aren't ready for change then God can't give you what you need nor get you where you need to be. We miss out on our blessings when we don't allow the process of change to take place.

Change is a lifestyle that we have to adopt to function for the rest of our existence. Renewing the spirit and mind isn't easy, but it is what we must do! It will produce the person that God sees as the final product. What I mean is when God change Simon name to Peter. He changed his name because of the confession of Jesus as the Messiah. What I spoken before about our truths and imperfections, confess to make us better. Change is for the better, unless it goes against the word of God.

Everyone has goals. Each one of us has to change our mindsets or point of view to reach those goals. Life changing events brings us to a choice of making new goals. Accomplishing those goals brings change. An example is my marriage was rocky. We didn't live together. I wanted him to be a certain way. I didn't look at myself. I asked God what was I doing wrong? The word of God says "Ask, and it will be given to you; seek, and you will find; knock, and it will be opened to you" (Matthew 7:7, KJV). Once, I open the doors to see the answers that God was giving me and accept it! God gave me, my heart desire was to publish this book. Now, I am stronger, wiser, more knowledgeable, and understanding to people concerns, needs or situations.

The process of change that God takes us through sometimes is to teach us how to love. Love is simple! Love is action. "For this is the love of God, that we keep His commandments. And His commandments are not burdensome" (1John 5:3, KJV). The word of God says love isn't burdensome. Change is really burdensome. It is God's love for us. As I stated before God is looking at the final product.

"For as he thinketh in his heart, so is he" (Proverbs 23:7, KJV), we as the people of God think too low of ourselves. We have so many family members, friends or the world make us feel we don't deserve better things in life. Our God is rich! He has mansions. His words say "But my God shall supply all your need according to his riches in glory by Christ Jesus" (Philippians 4:19, KJV). We know our God is rich! When are we going to realized that our God is rich! First, we should do whatever He ask of us. He knows what we are in need of in this changing process. Rather, changing your mindset, a car to make it easier to complete a goal, or doing the things of God. We first must ask, and it will be given to you, seek and you will find, knock and it will be opened to you" (Matthew 7:7, KJV). Once, we complete that instruction, then we have to have faith. Faith is action. "But without faith it is impossible to please him" (Hebrews 11:6, KJV), we don't realize we have not pleased God because we don't have faith. Faith isn't this big mansion on the hill. God said we have faith the size of a mustard seed. He will move! If you want to change have faith and apply the word of God.

ACKNOWLEDGING THE CHANGE

What is God purpose for me? What area of your life do you need to change? What are your imperfections? How do I reach my purpose? What are my goals? What are the steps to get there?

An example you might say I am selfish. Acknowledgement is step one, step two, read the word of God to see what it says about being selfish. Third, take a step, which could be volunteer at the soup kitchen once a month.

Acknowledge:

_____

_____

_____

_____

_____

_____

_____

_____

_____

Scripture(s) to apply:

_____

_____

_____

_____

_____

_____

_____

_____

_____

What steps God has given you to take:

_____

_____

_____

_____

_____

_____

_____

_____

_____

_____

_____

_____

_____

_____

_____

_____

_____

_____

_____

_____

_____

_____

_____

_____

_____

_____

_____

_____

_____

_____

NEGATIVITY: TAUGHT, THOUGHT & TALKED

Negativity is defined as (adjective) expressing or containing negation or denial, refusing consent, as to a proposal, expressing refusal to do something, (noun) a negative statement, answer, word, gesture, etc., a refusal of assent. Negativity is based off the word negative. As research on defining negative, this word is an adjective, noun and adverb (Dictionary.com). This is a display of how many different forms of negativity can come in presenting itself.

Negative used as an adjective describes expressing one's feelings, such as refusal and assent. Compared to negative used as a noun it is a thing, which is a statement, answer, word, gesture. Negative as an adverb is a phrase or group of words that modifies or qualifies an adjective, verb, or another adverb or a word group, expressing a relation of place, time, circumstances, manner, cause, degree, etc. You may ask what is all this information concerning adjectives, nouns and adverbs has to do with what I am trying to tell you about negativity. The key words are expressing, it causes people most of the time to say whatever they are feeling. Some people handle situations of life or life challenges according to their feelings. Their feelings take them on a path that is dark. An apology can't fix what had or has been done. An example of that is a tornado comes through and tear the roof off your house. You can't live in the house. You have to find somewhere to go. If you have insurance on the home. You call to get the process started, then see what can be salvaged. I hope you see what your feelings can do. Sometimes it can be fixed, but if it can't you have to deal with the consequences.

This quote defines negativity in the spiritual form. "Negativity in the spiritual world is darkness, that is toxic, cause anger, bitterness and hate. It has been known to change a person's perception of a situation or outcome" (Kim Parker, 2020).

Now, that I have broken down negativity to bite size pieces. I want you to understand how much power within yourself to change this negative into positive. Let's begin with discussing taught.

TAUGHT

All of us grew up in different environments with different information programmed into our souls through the conscious and subconscious mind. This input from those around us, such as family, friends and church family. They determine how we think for the rest of our lives. Our homes of course, the primary environment, that is our parents. Our parents taught us the way we think today. Most of them did not realize they were teaching us how to think negative. As we grew up, the end result of our attitudes and behaviors turns negative.

Our parents are our first teachers to the classroom called life. They are to teach us how to think, problem solve, take care of a household, etc. When the time came, we were ready to put to work what we have learned. In my case, it was what my parents said and did. For others it was how your parents acted. How you going to teach me Christian values. When I need them the most, I get negativity? Our parents aren't bad or trying to do anything wrong. They just believe negative things. They are using what they were taught from their parents. They can't give you what they didn't receive. An example if you go to the store, you need a gallon of milk. The store is completely out of gallon of milk. It only has one half of gallon left. This is our parents giving us as children what we need. We have to search for the rest in the word of God, and pray to be led to the right person. Your parents believe that what they are feeding, you is positive. Reality it is negative, the question is how do you rise above that?

"Now the God of patience and consolation grant you to be likeminded one toward another according to Christ Jesus: that ye may with one mind and one mouth glorify God even the Father of our Lord Jesus Christ" (Romans 15:5-6, KJV). These two verses are saying that God has the patience and counseling to teach us how to be positive. God will send the people to teach you how to be like minded. Like-minded is an adjective. Adjectives should describe or say who we are. Like-minded is define as having similar tastes or opinions (Google). This is the mindset of God. When you have a positive mindset, you bring that same vibe you have, to those people you meet who are positive, they can teach you ways to improve yourself. Teach you how to speak to the imperfections. As I stated before, acknowledging your imperfections is the beginning to teaching yourself to move from negative to positive. When you say anything negative about yourself or someone else. You need to say seven positive things to break the course of negativity. Once you start teaching yourself how to overcome the negativity you have been taught. Let's retrain your thoughts.

THOUGHT

Sometimes we think less of ourselves than we should. We don't have the encouragement. We didn't receive the attention, feel like others don't care. You have to change how you think. Our thinking is our thoughts. Thoughts is defined as the product of mental activity; that which one thinks, a single act or product of thinking; idea or notion, the act or process of thinking; mental activity, the capacity or faculty of thinking, reasoning imaging, etc., a consideration or reflection, or mediation contemplation, or recollection.

As thoughts has been defined, we now know that the way you're taught is the answer to your thoughts. You know that the way you were taught is wrong but like-minded is of God. Your thoughts have to be of God also. Philippian 4:8 say "Finally, brethren, whatsoever things are true, whatsoever things are honest, whatsoever things are just, whatsoever things are pure, whatsoever things are lovely, whatsoever things are of good report; if there be any virtue, and if there be any praise, think on these things." These things are positive thoughts. An example is you may live in a place with roaches. It isn't because you don't keep you house clean. May be the tenants that had the place before you were not clean. You might not have the finances to purchase a terminator. Well, complaining, whining doesn't make it better. How about you look at the positive. The positive is I am not homeless, I have a roof over my head, I have a job that pays all my bills, etc. Another example is someone gets a new car. You may need a car. Don't get jealous. That isn't of God. Instead celebrate them, even sow into that person with the new car. Give them ten dollars of gas money or buy a gas gift card. Sowing into that person blessing will cause God to bless you.

The things that have been instill from your parents that were negative. A positive person will teach you how to break that curse and generational curses. This what the word of God speaks of consolation and patience. He or she will take time to teach you as you enter each form of life challenges. The first person that taught me how to break the negativity was Pastor Marlene Chisolm. She took the time and taught me to apply the word of God. When negative situations happen, she would give me the word and pray with me. Eventually, I got stronger and stronger. I would speak the word over myself. Another life situation happened that the enemy broke my family. I didn't know what way to turn. I prayed and cried. Pastor Chisolm and I would still pray. My husband went on searching to help us through the situation. The negativity that I felt, heard, thought and said to me. It was crushing me, to second guess myself so much, that I didn't see myself in a positive mindset. Here comes a lifetime family friend. Never thought our paths would cross again. Co-Pastor, Singer, Business Owner, and much more Bonita Burney Simmons showed and taught me along with her lovely mother Ms. Rose. These power house women of God, taught me how to look at the positive in a situation that at the time I thought I wasn't going to make it through. As I continued to think I wasn't going to make it. I continued to lean on God. I delighted myself in God so much that God carried me through the word of God says acknowledge him in all thy ways (Proverbs 3:5 NKJV). I did just that! When your thoughts are on that, you know how to respond to negativity. When you learn how to respond to negativity you are ready to talk.

TALK

Once you get taught, your thoughts under control into your routine vocabulary. Your talk begins to follow into the place. "Giving thanks always for all things unto God and the Father in the name of our Lord Jesus Christ" (Ephesian 5:20 NKJV). This scripture says give thanks. What it means is in a time of a pandemic. A lot of people are out of work, lost homes, or dealing with death of a love one, friend, parent, etc. You have to speak good. You have to tell God thank you for my roof over my head. Even though it may not have heat or in the best conditions. Tell God thank you that I am alive to feel the pains in your body. Your job got shut down due to someone catching the Corona virus. You have to work from home. Thank God you have to work from home. Thank God you are able to still work and have a home to work from. No, you may not like the fact it is from home. Be thankful! We have been blessed so much until we are spoiled. We have taken the small things for granted, such as physical, mental, and spiritual. We forget to be thankful for the trees, birds, the sun and the grass. Be thankful is shown in our talk. The next time someone says why you so positive or thankful. Tell them I remember where God has brought me from.

NEGATIVE

What are you negative about? Is it a person? Your job? Whatever it maybe, write it down below. If you are not aware you are negative. Write your acknowledgements as you are aware.

Here is an example:

Negative: a co-worker Peggy – she is nosy

Positive: She can dress well.

Negative:

_____

_____

_____

Positive:

_____

_____

_____

Negative:

_____

_____

_____

Positive:

_____

_____

_____

RECOGNIZE IT, REPROGRAM

We see that you have learned the basics of how to recognize negativity. We notice how negativity comes in different forms. Now, we have to keep others with negative comments from contaminating your spirit. You have to keep the negativity of this world from contaminating your spirit, along with acknowledging other negative things you may see and hear. The question is how do I keep these things out? The key is the word of God and your mind.

"And be not conformed to this world: but be ye transformed by the renewing of your mind, that ye may prove what is that good, and acceptable and perfect, will of God" (Romans 12:2 KJV). This scripture teaches you how to recognize it and them reprogram your thoughts. An example your job made a change to your hours. Others may complain about how their hours are cut or how they going to make it, etc. You have to look at the positive that you have a job. Instead of agreeing, you get quiet or tell that person to look at the positive. You have a job!

These steps to reprogram helps you to become like minded as we discussed earlier. Another scripture used to reprogram is "casting down imaginations, and every high thing that exalteth itself against the knowledge of God, and bringing into captivity every thought to the obedience of Christ" (2 Corinthians 10:5 KJV). As things pop into your mind, you have to know what is of God. You must know what isn't of God. This scripture will help you reprogram your mind and thoughts.

Here are the steps to recognize and reprogram:

1. Be aware

    You have to be aware what is coming out of your mouth. The word of God says, life and death is in the power of our tongue. Let us be watchful of our words.

2. Speak it

    When you are aware, you begin to speak what is of God. We see the change the positive take place as the like minded as we speak of in Romans 15:5-6 and Romans 12:2.

3. Set Atmosphere

    When you have taken the first step of being aware this is the beginning of setting your atmosphere. The positivity is come to you. You have to correct and remove any negativity that attempts to come in your atmosphere. Visually you may not see it right away. Spiritually you feel energized, free and happiness that only God can give even when you are having life challenges and trials. You will see the Romans 4:17 KJV "and calleth those things which be not as though they were."

Let's begin to reprogram!

REPROGRAM

What have you recognized through your day? What was something someone said that you had to correct to set your atmosphere? As you write each thought/ memory. Write the scripture that goes with correcting the atmosphere.

Example: Recognize: Co-worker said she gives up on doing good.

Reprogram: Galatians 6:9 KJV And let us not be weary in well doing: for in due season we shall reap, if we faint not.

Recognize:

_____

_____

_____

_____

Reprogram:

_____

_____

_____

_____

Recognize:

_____

_____

_____

_____

Reprogram:

_____

_____

_____

_____

POSITIVITY

I stated earlier that you have to recognize it and reprogram it. When you are in life challenges that doesn't look hopeful. How do you see the positive?

That is a good question. Romans 7:21 KJV says "I find then a law, that, when I would do good, evil is present with me." The scripture, Romans 15:5-6 states how God wants us to have the like-minded mindset. Well, what if you are someone who isn't in the same mindset as you? If you are in that situation, you have to look to God. When you look to God, you will see the positive. An example is that you can have a challenging day at work. It could be that your supervisor is constantly calling you to do this before you can finish one project. Supervisor may be stressed out and takes it out on you all that day. The positive is that you still showed him or her respect, you may help someone else by watching you showing kindness to your supervisor, and just the fact that you made it through another day in with your peace of mind. These are positives, that don't seem like a lot. It is a lot to be thankful to God. Then you have days that everywhere you turn it is chaos and tragedy. This where you look in the Bible. God gives you that one scripture. If you are seasoned, God will bring that one scripture from your heart. The tears will flow, a wave of your hand, a thank you Jesus will fill your spirit. My favorite you rocking in your chair. If you have a work place where you might can't do any of what I just spoke of. You find grass or a tree look at God's creation. God's creation will give you joy because you that same power lives inside of me. What make it even better I can cast all my cares on him.

I know all I just said sounds so simple. It is do the work to change your mindset (taught), thoughts, and talk. When you keep positivity in the atmosphere the problems of life don't frustrate you. You give them to God!

POSITIVITY

The negative activity we did earlier, this activity is going to be reversed. The first question, what did he or she do to you or wrong towards others? The second question, what did you do? The third question, what biblical character did you show or act out? The fourth question, how or where did you see the positive in, through or at the end of the day?

1. _____
   _____
   _____
   _____

2. _____
   _____
   _____
   _____

3. _____
   _____
   _____
   _____

4. _____
   _____
   _____
   _____

SPENDING TIME WITH GOD

Some people do not know how to spend time with God. They don't know what God voice sound like. They don't know when God is speaking to him or her. Some people say they mediate. Some watch the beauty of God's creation. Whatever is your way…. this keeps the positivity stronger and the spirit renewed each day.

Life challenges turns into a storm of life. Sometimes we make a storm because we can't wait on God to fix it. During times like this we need to spend time with God to keep our minds at peace. God is your protection, peace, joy, happiness. He is our source to help others as well as yourself. When people hurt me or speak evil things against me, spending time with God would reveal those things who the people are, and circumstances to you. Life can keep us so busy that we forget to spend time with God. God should be our first priority. Things or persons shouldn't be over God. He is the one who created man or woman to give us these inventions. Why not serve the man who is above all. I think it makes sense to me.

Someone may ask how do I spend time with God? How do I hear from God? How do I know it is God speaking to me? Those are good questions. The first question is how do I spend time with God? Spending time with God is just like giving yourself that quiet time before the kids get up for school or before your husband gets up for work. You get something positive like a scripture. You mediate on that scripture. An example is the scripture "Jesus wept" (John 11:35, KJV). As you mediate on that scripture throughout the day. God may reveal how he cried for us. He cried because of all the sin we have committed. Jesus his good self, sacrifice his life for us so we can have a personal relationship with him. The Israelites had to sacrifice goats, birds, etc. just for God to forgive them of their sins. All we have to do is ask for forgiveness. Just as your grandmother or your parents would say "don't do it again". Some of us go right back and do it again. We do it again in another way. That topic is for another day. This is a way of spending time with God. God speaks to you about his word. You listen. Your question may be what does God voice sound like? His voice is a calm, strong, assuring and positive. Where the enemy can sound make himself sound that way as well. The results are negative. We all experience that voice to say hit, slap, or stab someone. That isn't God! You may say that is someone who has mental health issues. The enemy in this day and time is trying to destroy the people on God's earth. COVID-19 was God knocking at our door of our hearts. He said "look to him". We have seen that material things can be taken away in a blink of an eye with COVID-19. James 4:14 KJV "Whereas ye know not what shall be on the morrow. For what is your life? It is even a vapour, that appeareth for a little time, and then vanisheth away. We have seen love ones here one minute and gone the next. This is how to cherish the lives of others. We are a vapour. What are you putting out into the atmosphere?

Second question is how do I hear from God? What I mentioned earlier about mediating on scripture is one way to hear from God. God works in many ways! He may have one word to stand out to you in that whole chapter or scripture. Once you define that word or words. You will see what God is telling us. The next powerful way to hear from God is praying. Prayer is our way we talk to God. God talks to us as well. It may be spontaneous. An example, have you been driving and all of a sudden you want ice cream. So, you stop! You receive your order, you may see someone that has been on your mind for some days. Then they share with you what is going on with them. Well, this is a form of hearing God voice or a move of God. What I stated earlier is a combine answer to the third question. Oh! My favorite God will have you to do something that may seem crazy to the world system of thinking. The scripture says But God hath chosen the foolish things of the world to confound the wise; and God hath chosen the weak things of the world to confound the things which are mighty (1 Corinthians1:27, KJV). Yet this may sound stupid to others and sometimes crazy to us. When we complete the assignment. God leaves us in awe. Mostly that we were so obedient and overcame fear. Fear causes us to be disobedient which isn't of God. As parents, you have that child that you can ask him or her to do something. You don't have to check to see if it is completed. This is how obedience is seen in God eyes. He wants to bless us. We miss it because of our disobedience. Well, you ask how spending time with God got to do with this. The time you spend or has spent with God allow you to hear the voice of God. This will give you the instructions that God want us to complete. Completing these instructions is obedience. Obedience leads us to the blessings of God. That is priceless!

Another great factor of spending time with God is revealing things to you. Sometimes it isn't time for you to say what it is. God is just that awesome. His word says "But when thou doest alms, let not thy left hand know what thy right hand doeth" (Matthew 6:3, KJV). I looked up alms. Alms means money or food given to poor people. We aren't supposed to let people know what we do for others. We should just do it! It is required of us we are small gods. When we are made in the image of God. We are a god. We were created to up lift, encourage, give, feed the hungry, sow into others. Jesus did all of this while he was here on earth. Spending time with God will show us each day how to minister to our husband, children, family members and others we come into contact. You don't know who you just saved.

SPENDING TIME WITH GOD

"I love them that love me; and those that seek me early shall find me" (Proverbs 8:17, KJV). It is best to spend time with him early in the morning. Things seem calmer in the morning. If we go back to the book of Genesis. "In the beginning God created the heaven and the earth" (Genesis 1:1 KJV). God created it all! Spending time with God gives you a fulfillment that is priceless. It makes you a better person. "And God said, Let there be light: and there was light." (Genesis 1:3, KJV). When you spend time with God, you are the light to others. You know how people say that I just love being around you. This is why because your relationship with God shows.

Below write down what God has shared with you. Was it a revelation, what to do for a person, a business idea, a process of how to go about a person, business, church, ministry, etc.?

Scripture: _____

_____

_____

_____

_____

_____

_____

Revelation: _____

_____

_____

_____

_____

_____

_____

_____

_____

_____

_____

_____

_____

_____

Church/Ministry: _____

_____

_____

_____

_____

_____

_____

_____

_____

_____

_____

_____

_____

_____

_____

_____

_____

_____

_____

Business(es): _____

_____

_____

_____

_____

_____

STEPS TO RENEW THE MIND

We just mentioned the very first step to all the answers to life and in this book is spending time with God. When life gets you where the enemy distracts you. Distractions from the enemy are serious. Sometimes so serious it may cause you your life. If you are not paying attention, the enemy knows God has great things in store for you. Keep your eyes on God so you can call the snake a snake. Here are some steps to get back on track.

1. We must depend on God!

    This is the first step to renewing the mind. Renewing the mind takes more than knowledge, more than psychology and human effort. It takes the work of the Lord. Jesus is the One who gives us the ability to change.

2. We must have a desire to change.

    You shouldn't change because someone else wants you to change. You must want to change because it makes you better. It will improve your quality of life.

3. We must increase our knowledge of life.

    I mentioned in step two, improve your quality of life. Your improvement of the quality of life do have an effect on others. What we know helps others to improve.

4. We must be diligently applying these truths and knowledge to our daily lives.

   An example of how to do that is when life situations occur. We must have an open mind. An open mind is reading the word of God and applying it to the situation that you are dealing with each day or moment. You will see the hand of God work out the situation.

5. We must defend our new state of mind.

   Fight against our old ways of thinking and limitations people want to place on you. An example is when you share certain things with a friend or family member. Their comments are negative, in the sense of the comment "why you want to do that?", "you can't do that?", "how are you going to do that? You can barely pay your bills."

   When you hear these comments like that! You have to dissociate yourself from them. This is how you are defending your state of mind. Another example is you may feel sick. Someone might say "you have cancer". You have to rebuke that! You speak the word of God. This brings in the positive energy that we mentioned earlier in the book.

6. We need to dissociate ourselves from some of the people from our past.

   This means to stop communicating with these friends or associates. If they aren't to help you then cut them off. Oh! You have those who are willing to help as long it is something he or she is getting something out of it. Prepare yourself to cut them off with a strategy.

These steps will help you to keep the positive atmosphere. It is important to keep your mind on Jesus.

INSPIRATIONAL POEMS

By

Carla Mewborn

&

Edit

Mellanie Brown

THINGS IN LIFE

Carla Mewborn

Things go wrong in life

Hope and faith makes us strive

It is the thread

That help us sail through

Faith is a power we can't see

A spiritual blueprint to how we overcome

Life challenges

Faith is life of the unknown future

Hold on to your faith

It is the anchor of your life

FAITH IN HEART

Carla Mewborn

Faith is in your heart

Forgetting those failures from the start

It is all because of hope

That your heart can scope

If faith is in your heart

When someone has done you wrong

Don't depart

Keep your hope high

And you will get the answers to your why

Being faithful in your heart!

MY SPECIAL FRIEND

Carla Mewborn

Isn't it funny?

How some people don't realize

They are special

In the sight of others

They are thoughtful

Without even thinking about it

They are there when you need them

They share their time without anything in return

Always giving in some form or another

It's lovely how these people teach us

So much about living

You are that special person

Thank you for being my friend

STRONG WOMAN VS. WOMAN OF STRENGTH

Carla Mewborn

A strong woman exercises each day

This keeps her body in shape

She isn't afraid of her fears

She doesn't let anyone get the best of her

A woman of strength gives

Her best to everyone

She makes mistakes

Avoids making them again in the future

She realizes that it is wisdom

One of God's blessings

That capitalizes a better life

AUTHOR BIOS

Carla Mewborn is a wife, mother and grandmother. She is active in her local church and community. She is a resident of New Bern, North Carolina.

Printed in the United States
by Baker & Taylor Publisher Services